Get All A's in the Game of Life

Insights Along the Way

Mother's Edition

Brought to you by
IdentityMagazine.net

Get All A's in the Game of Life
Insights Along the Way
Mother's Edition

An IdentityMagazine.net Book

Edited By:
Susan Vernicek, Creator of IdentityMagazine.net
+ Kimberly Sauve, Editor

Copyright © 2020
ISBN: 978-1-64871-388-0

Back Cover Photo: Pink Flamingo Photography
Cover Design By Elena Suster

Published by:
CJS Identity Properties, LLC
PO Box 36
Shawnee on Delaware, PA 18356
www.IdentityMagazine.net

Published and Print On Demand through IngramSpark

I'd like to express my appreciation for all of you who have shared your wisdom, advice, tips, and funny stories to support other moms on the journey of motherhood.

Without my family, friends, colleagues, readers, clients, and students, I wouldn't be where I am today. You all have supported me for over a decade as I evolved from working 9-5.

I was a depressed young woman who struggled to find true happiness, abundance, and acceptance of choices and responsibility. Over the years my identity has surely strengthened, not just as a woman, but as an entrepreneur, friend, daughter, sibling, colleague, wife, and mother. I never thought I'd find a husband and babies in a baby carriage.

I thank you from the bottom of my heart.

I love and appreciate you.

Table of Contents

"Love is possible whenever you're ready to receive it."

—*Susan Vernicek, Mom of twins*

Foreword

Whoever said motherhood was the hardest job on the planet, hit the mark.

Somehow, millions upon millions of women openly offer their entire lives for unlimited years, without a thought of personal rewards, the impact of being sleep deprived for decades, or the endless personal sacrifices made for the betterment of others.

It's both the absolute best decision we have ever made and the one that can bring us to our knees, head to hands.

Only Mothers can truly understand the joys and heartaches of motherhood. The special ones are preparing for the role of motherhood years before giving birth or completing the adoption papers.

Susan is one of the special ones.

I had the privilege of knowing Susan long before she married and brought her two amazing twins into the world. She has been on a mission for decades nurturing and caring for all the people in her life— even the ones she never actually met. Susan has always been a nurturer, from hosting fundraisers for her 30th birthday to enthusiastically helping me launch my women's empowerment organization B.I.G. more than a dozen years ago.

Susan has an almost magical way of supporting the Mothers of the world. She intuitively knows when Mothers need a lift—especially after offering their last bit of energy after an exhaustingly long day. She knows first-hand the defeating feeling Mothers can experience when their best efforts can be undervalued by those they love.

Susan's latest gift to mothers is this very special compilation of mothers' insights and life observations. This joy-filled book is compiled of page after page of comforting, funny, compassionate and heartfelt messages from one mother to another.

I urge you to embrace these daily doses of recognition that Mothers everywhere so greatly deserve.

Tara Gilvar, President and Owner of B.I.G.
Believeinspiregrow.com

About Identity

The Identity Mission

Identity is a digital magazine that empowers women to transform through Self-Acceptance, Appreciation, and Personal Achievement—Get All A's™. Through a community of writers, experts, influencers and bloggers, our mission is to help women get all A's in the game of life by discovering their power of Self-Acceptance, Appreciation, and Personal Achievement. We believe that once you accept a situation or circumstance and you show gratitude and appreciation for what you currently have, it is then that you can achieve at a great and more connected level within yourself and your life.

The Identity Experience

We are all individuals in our thoughts, interests, beliefs, and experiences. Each of us harbors our own fears, doubts, questions, and insecurities. That's why we bring you a positive and safe place to turn to for information, inspiration, support, sharing, and permission to just be who you are. We allow you to be perfectly imperfect.

You won't find articles on our website about the latest

and greatest diets, fashion fads, celebrity chatter, and beauty miracles. Why? Because there's enough of that in the world, and we understand that there is no healthy quick fix when it comes to your mental or physical health. The full identity experience allows you to embrace your inner self, to love who you currently are, and to achieve your potential without comparison to anyone else. Our articles and insights reflect these important philosophies of self-love and self-help.

The Identity Woman — You!

Whether you're a wife, mother, student, entrepreneur, business professional, teacher, or artist, you are the Identity woman. You're strong and intelligent, funny and curious, ambitious and outgoing, and open to new ideas that will make a worthwhile difference in your life and the lives of others. You're caring and nurturing, often more focused on home and work obligations than you are on yourself. You go all day, yet can't resist the urge to curl up on the couch with a good movie or book. Separate from that, you're a woman with moments of discontent, like us all, and at times feel less than self-confident and alone in your concerns. You need a place to reach out. Identity provides that safe space.

Identity is designed by women and for women. It's a wellness community for those of us who have no interest in feeling inferior while looking at the airbrushed and enhanced cover girls or social media posts that dominate our media, and who we sometimes feel compelled to emulate. The Identity woman doesn't want to be constantly reminded of who she's not— she wants to know that who she currently is, is far more than enough.

The Identity Butterfly

We embrace the butterfly as a symbol of our uniqueness and the personal journey each of us travels. Not one butterfly looks alike, and this is a reminder that we don't need to compare ourselves to anyone else because we are talented and beautiful just the way we are. Like our own identities, a butterfly morphs through many stages and layers during its lifetime. The changes we face—day in and day out—help shape our identities into the multiple layers that make us who we are. Our identities are made up of our physical, mental, and spiritual selves, as well as our hobbies, religious beliefs, education, intelligence, and distinct viewpoints. We embrace the belief that our identities run far deeper than what can be seen on the surface.

The Identity Community

We invite you into our community of women who are eager to support you and learn from you. In our community, we celebrate the real layers that make us each distinct, and we share our personal experiences and personal stories. Identity is not a place where you will leave feeling like you need to change, but a safe haven for women who desire to evolve and become stronger through the support of others.

The Identity Community is composed of readers and writers who spark rich discussions and learn from one another. We're always looking for women to join our team of writers and share their tips and advice with our audience.

Why & How To Use This Book

The Why:
Rooting for Your Success

In the **Mother's Edition of Get All A's in the Game of Life,** we offer words brought forth from a diverse group of Mothers for the purpose of nurturing and motivating you ever forward. It is our hope that this book of quotes and other useful tidbits becomes a source of fuel and comfort: a wellspring from which any Mother can draw upon over and over—that is, inspiration, invigoration, advice, nods of recognition, and, at times, laughter. The original quotes and anecdotes that pepper these pages—some poignant, others informative, many compassionate—can serve to validate, strengthen, and elevate you.

This book was conceived as a tailored tool to help optimize your journey as a mother and a master multi-tasker via lessons learned and paths taken by none other than your fellow moms. It appears at your fingertips to read, refer to, repeat and relay.

The How:
Embracing the Words

Read: So, go ahead and read—swiftly or at your leisure. Either way, we highly recommend that you bookmark your favorite quotes as you peruse these pages. Make note of quotes that resonate with you. Highlight excerpts that elicit thought or emotion, that guide or reassure, and quotes that simply pique your interest. Recognize ideas that sync with your personality or relate to your circumstances to give a try and implement into your life.

Paste, post, share, repeat: Here's when the goin' gets good: Now you can begin to embrace the true spirit of Get All A's in the Game of Life...and benefit to the fullest.

Select those quotes that speak to you, that really hit home. We're referring to the insights, and advice that guide, revitalize, and soothe as well as the words that bring about confidence, courage, and joy. Next, jot them down and tape them onto walls, mirrors, computer screens, refrigerators, lamps, and dashboards. Better yet, recite them with pride, either to yourself or out loud. Celebrate YOURSELF with affirmative quotes as you face the vibrant (yet occasionally self-doubting) champion in the mirror. Dispense yourself a hefty dose of motherhoods' quotes first thing in the morning to ensure an 'I CAN DO' attitude! Remind yourself that these are articulations that have already backed and bettered like-minded mothers.

We didn't create this book of quotes just to look pretty. The quotes on these pages are available for you to be empowered and to share. Leverage the connectivity of the internet to plant these seeds of empowerment among your "mom sisters". Text or email your favorite quotes or ideas to those who will appreciate them. Add an engaging and uplifting image and post them on social media. Share these expressions and assertions to SUPPORT other mothers, as well as the originators of these quotes, completing a full circle of empowerment.

We will all testify that no one individual succeeds solo. You know the saying, "It takes a village..." Support from others throughout the entirety of our ventures is indispensable. Guidance, encouragement, and enlightenment are crucial to the undertaking that is motherhood. We are confident that this book of quotes and wisdom will ultimately underscore the vast power and potential of every mother who reads it—as well as those with whom she shares it.

"Ask for help. Accept and understand that motherhood takes a village—and help is not a sign of weakness, it's a sign of courage and strength."

—Susan Vernicek, Mom of Twins

Chapter One

Practice Acceptance

Receive and Acknowledgement

Accept and you shall receive: a spin-off of the familiar, although just as much a cliché, we're stickin' with it. In order to flourish, the devoted Mother must begin at the beginning—whether wanted, not wanted, or not ready. In any circumstance, the moment you find out you're a mother or going to be a mother, an acknowledgement and acceptance must be made. It also means accepting oneself and one's circumstances at the current moment in time.

Born of self-awareness, amplified with self-love, and paired with lack of criticism and negative judgment, acceptance emerges. Let's embrace and cherish all that is positive along with, well...the "neutrals." Place them in the forefront of the mind. Cradle and cultivate these qualities and conditions. As for that term "acceptance," we're not talking about passivity or bowing our heads in resignation. And disappointments? Well, we need to admit those, too. The quotes in this chapter speak to these same notions: receipt and acknowledge the enormous potential for positive change. Because the future lies ahead, wide open, to bear out the goals and dreams we envision and are working so diligently to meet.

Surely acceptance is a fundamental component within a process: a decidedly challenging one for many women, especially Mothers. It first entails purposeful reflection. We need to face that mirror—look into our authentic selves and ask some serious questions. Identify our values, virtues, morals, and beliefs. Unearth those talents, passions, and visions. Get to know ourselves inside and out. Love our "selves." Allow and simultaneously own our worth, our might, and our extensive capabilities.

Next, we need to recognize our circumstances, from family to financial to logistical and more—the whole shebang, the entire gestalt. Distinguish the ideally independent women that we are today with a fine-tuned sense of where we'd like to be in the future. Imagine how we can arrive there in motherhood and in all of life. In this way, we also begin to define what success means to each of us.

Only when we discover our realities can we harness the qualities that constitute our identities, in order to truly acknowledge our powers of adequacy. And only when we comprehend what lies before us can we transform any perceived negatives into forces with which the world will reckon. We take responsibility for ourselves, recreating life along each of our journeys of motherhood.

As the following quotes illustrate, acceptance begets growth. Owning and embracing our truths in the NOW becomes the base from which our journey will push forward. In other words, we accept what is to work with what we've got; build upon it to progress; and, subsequently we soar. As we ride the motherhood rollercoaster—managing our identities, children, careers, relationships and everything in be-tween—once these insights gel, well, we're golden and the feeling is pure, real, and ALIVE.

My Motherhood Rollercoaster

Oh, I'm so glad to have you here and thank you for picking up this quote book. Motherhood is no joke, right? It's an emotional rollercoaster that I'm blessed to have——but sometimes I struggle to embrace all the ups and downs. At the time of my writing this, my twins, June and Cade are five and half years old and push every button, especially the patience button all the dang time! I can tell you right now from experience the one thing I'm constantly and consciously working on is my resistance. I've come a long way with learning to accept the situation at hand or the circumstance we may be in, quicker than I was as a new mom.

Meaning, I've learned to stop questioning and resisting change, effort, or struggle in the moment than a few days later after scrutiny of some sort. I've learned to have the understanding that anything is possible and nothing can faze me anymore, LOL. Right? Poop on the walls, baby powder all over the bathroom, throwing my back out when I'm making the top bunk bed, or falling down the stairs while carrying the 10th load of laundry down to the laundry room. *It's chaos. Right?*

And as I sit here and laugh while I remember all of these moments so vividly, I'm blessed and grateful.

I've experienced an ugly miscarriage and soon

after I was pregnant with twins. I'll never take it for granted, and although I'm not perfect, I'm giving my best each and every day with the knowledge and resources I have at hand. I'm sure you're doing the exact same thing and we're in this together.

I know I'm not the only mother who's locked herself in the bathroom breaking down in tears or screaming to let out that feeling of being so overwhelmed, exhausted, and frustrated all at once.

I'm not the only mom that has wanted to run away because I didn't think I could handle being a great parent. I'm not the only mom who's questioned the path of marriage and having a family and trying to nurse twins at 4 in the morning while my husband sleeps the night away.

That's why this "Mother's Edition" is the 2nd in my quote book series. It's the most relatable for me, just like the first "Entrepreneur Edition", because these two very important and challenging areas of my life can feel suffocating, scary, and lonely at times.

I do believe and am proud I've found my truth, my balance and very, very seldom fall into the comparison trap that creates so much internal drama. I had to let go and urge you to do the same. You will never mother as another; you will be your own beautiful, perfectly imperfect mother.

So I hope this book provides comfort, validation, humor, and support for you as you take on your very own motherhood rollercoaster and strive for your Mom A-Game.

I've spent over a decade implementing the practices that I teach through my magazine, speaking, workshops, online programs, and books. I invite you to open your mind and heart and welcome all of the love from all of the moms who are here to support and uplift you whenever you need it.

I invite you to implement my "Get All A's" thought-provoking formula into your day-to-day so that you can release yourself from resistance, fear, or any un-serving thoughts and feelings. As a woman and a mother, when you can overcome a negative emotion or feeling within minutes and ground yourself, you're transforming in that moment and that allows you to break through, feel darn good, and achieve over and over.

Now, let's get started with our first A in the A-Game...
Self-Acceptance.

I'd love to give you a space right now, here within this book. What have you accepted within motherhood, physically and/or mentally? Additionally, what are you still working on accepting? Now, we're not talking about resignation, rather stepping into, embraced, and owned acceptance.

Stop + Think

"My advice for you in those struggling moments is to stop and think before you react to any situation. Children want to know that you care first before you lecture or tell them what you think. Always make sure they are OK, then talk to them and explain the right from wrong."

—*Sheryl White, Mom of 2*

Let Me Think About It

"Never say no first. I used to always say I'll think about it and usually another mother always said no first. Ha! So I didn't always have to be the bad guy."

—*Doris Vernicek, Mom of 3*

Everything Else Can Wait

"Always make sure your kids know you are there to listen whenever they need you. If they say they need to talk, drop what you're doing and put them first. Everything else can wait. Let them know they are the priority."

—*Laura Breiten, Mom of 3*

Faint of Heart

"Motherhood is not for the faint of heart. It tries you to your very soul. But, the benefits are thousandfold. We get to love another human being more than we could imagine. We witness growth (physical, emotional, spiritual) and guide with caring limits. We get to encourage individualism and cultivate gifts. I could fill the page with a full heart; but what I got was another chance to grow. I realize that I provided the best foundation possible and my job was to let go and let them soar."

—*Dawn Vernicek, Mom of 3*

Love

"My best wisdom is to love your family with all your being. Be firm, but nurture. Set boundaries with unconditional love and create a space of honesty and open-mindedness.

As a young girl, I didn't have a mother to guide me, teach me or listen to me for any part of my young childhood—no guidance or directions. Our father really did the best job he could have done raising four children. Thank the good Lord for my Baba; however she was from a completely different era as her own young adult growing up in the new world. When I finally went to move and live with my Mother states away from home, I was 18. Talk about a life lesson. I moved in with two complete strangers that I really didn't know. Living with my mother and Aunt, **my mom became my best friend. Her advice to me was always sharing her opinion and not TELLING me how to act or behave, but lead with guidance.** Living life in recovery and sobriety one day at a time, I have a life beyond my wildest dreams. I follow *The Four Agreements by Don Miguel Ruiz,* to always speak impeccably, which means without sin, never assume, never take things personal, and always do the best you can do."

—*Sandra Wagner, Mom of 2*

The Way That Works For You

"Do not fall into the rut of trying to be a perfect parent or comparing your child's development to another's. There is no one right way and every baby is different. It's just the way that works for you and yours. It may not be according to all the books, articles, blogs, or podcasts, and that's just fine."

—*Victoria Ronemus, Mom of 1*

Quality over Quantity

"It isn't about the quantity of time you spend with your children, it's about the quality of the time you spend."

—*Lynette Barbieri, Mom of 4*

Layers

"I've come to accept, own, and embrace every layer of motherhood and my identity. In doing so, my resistance to life and embracing who I am is lower. Meaning, I don't fight struggle, change, or being uncomfortable. With that, my heart and mind are more open for what's to come my way, and that makes the journey much more enjoyable."

—*Susan Vernicek, Mom of Twins*

I Don't Have All The Answers

"Acceptance is such a big part of motherhood. As a mom, I had to learn to accept that I don't have all of the answers, and that all I really have control over is loving my children every day. I learned to accept that I will make parenting mistakes, and that's O.K. because it's part of being human. I learned to accept that they are individual people with their own personalities, and while I can provide guidance, they will ultimately live their own lives and be who they were meant to be. I believe that the key to happiness as a parent is to accept and love my kids for who they are, not who I expected them to be."

—*Donna Leyens, Mom of 2*

Embrace Communication

"Don't be afraid to apologize to your child and ask for their help in knowing what to do. You may be very surprised at what they come up with. And don't try to control your child. Build cooperation. The more you try to control your child the more uncontrollable they will become, especially during those teens years. Work together to solve problems and establish a peaceful environment in your home."

—Dale L'Ecuyer, Mom of 5

Navigate the Aftermath

"Accept that you will mess up, that you'll get angry and lash out, that there will be moments or days where you will say to yourself, "So this is what my kid will be in therapy about in 20 years..." Take a deep breath and apologize to your little one (or big kid or teen). Turn it into an opportunity to show them what they are worth, what treatment they should expect, and how they in turn should handle it when they do something hurtful to another. Then, the hardest part—forgive yourself. You've taken a moment of anger and shown your child how to navigate the aftermath, shown them how to apologize and take responsibility. You are a wonderful mother!"

—Dori Eldridge Bell, Mom of 1

Accept Your Choice

"Everyone around is trying to act like experts; especially our mothers and grandmothers. They tell you what is best for your baby...but the truth is that ONLY YOU really know what your child needs! Because every child develops at its own pace and needs different things for its development. When someone denies what you are doing, listen to them, then do the research and see if it can be true. Ultimately, do what you think is right for you and your child."

—Zaneta Chylewska, Mom of 1

Nourished Over Perfection

"Having 3 kids in diapers under the age of 2 was insane. I quickly realized that I needed to say YES when people offered to help, even if my ego and pride wanted to say no. I also learned that perfection is overrated. It's much better to have 3 kids who are well nourished and happy, than to have the perfectly clean and organized house."

"Give yourself a break. You are doing great!"

—Elizabeth Girouard, Mom of 3

Endurance

"Life is full of small steps. Steps of joy, steps of feeling overwhelmed and even alone. The largest step of all is the step of endurance. The endurance that will take you through each platform of never ending love. Many steps of awe! As you watch your little ones become responsible loving parents. Motherhood then becomes a life cycle of many little steps."

—Dr. Monica Dunnagan, Mom of 2

Accept Change

"Being 45 and having a child certainly has its pros and cons! But certainly, most definitely, keeps you young! No one tells you how hard it is. My first few months felt like a blur...but reality set in and I realized that if I didn't take care of me, I would never be able to take care of my son. And so, yes, I changed....like "a lot" changed, and for the better. It is possible! When you think you figured out the patterns of your child, it changes, so go with the flow, and set your boundaries first."

—Jami Josephson Chace, Mom of 1

Guidance

"It's always great to have a support system and have people who can give you guidance when you are navigating the world of being a mom. But, remember to take it as guidance because in the end, you will know what is best for you and your child. Don't compare yourself to someone else's experience, because it is theirs, not yours. When you remember that, and keep remembering that, your insecurities will start to fade."

—Theresa Mary Hudzinski, Mom of 2

Slow Down

"Remember to slow down, breathe, hug them, and love them. You will miss this tomorrow. Don't get caught up in all the noise, you're right where you need to be, right now. I discovered this way too late so, I like to share it with parents who have little ones."

—Shauna Colicchio, Mom of 1

There is Always Grace

"Once is a mistake, twice is stupid! My kids have heard this come out of my mouth sooo many times! It makes them laugh to this day. It was my way of telling them and myself that there is always grace! You are allowed to make a mistake, but you should always try to learn from it! My boys knew they could come to me with any mistake and I would love them and help them figure out how not to be "stupid" and repeat it. But trust me, they would use that against me a lot! I had a habit of leaving the house and then having to run back in because I forgot something: my purse, my keys, etc.

I would often hear, "Once is a mistake and twice is stupid!" as soon as I would open the door. It became a running joke with me and my boys. Trust me, as a single mom of two boys, being able to laugh at mistakes in life was a survival tool! Allow your children and yourself the grace to not be perfect!"

—*Alison Last, Mom of 2*

Accepting & Owning Self-care

"For years, I prioritized everyone but myself. It took me years to realize that if my tank was empty, I was extremely ineffective. This pertained to parenting, being a wife, being a friend, serving on ministries and different committees, etc. I came to realize that I didn't have to "do it all," but rather pick a few things to do well. I began prioritizing my health—body, mind, and soul. It was a difficult shift because I sometimes felt guilty. Guilt of saying "no" to things, enduring negative comments from others, and the judging from others watching me take a step back and not committing to everyone and everything. I had to develop a tough exterior and mindset. Women can be extremely judgmental, and I needed to be "solid" in my decision and what was best for my mental health.

Now, I am quick to recognize when I'm exhausted and even identify the old mom going down the same path. A few years ago, I was depressed, stressed, drinking too much wine, and not very motivated. Changes needed to be made for my "mothering" and "myself" to be both productive and fruitful."

—Jaime Goulet, Mom of 2

Let Life Guide You

"It was a tough transition for the kids to start elementary school, while working a full-time office job. So much to think of, after school care, sick day care, summers, (2.5 month of coverage needed!) All the things that while in day care I did not need to think much about. I have learned over the years now to accept what I can plan and accept that life happens and at times I need to drop my daily routine to just be there for my kids. Almost always things work out. I try to be a planner, but with kids you accept that you sometimes just go with life and let it guide you."

—Amy McClellan, Mom of 2

Feel Powerful

"Simplify your thinking when it all becomes overwhelming. You can't solve it all at once. When you feel low, stop and ask yourself what is one thing you can do to make yourself feel better? What is one action you can take to combat your house. Take it one step at a time. If you feel low about your identity, start dressing yourself every day with the thought of how you feel when you look your best, nevermind if you actually have somewhere to go. Take control over simple changes or routines that you can do for your own self identity. When you feel powerful and great, life feels easier and more exciting."

—*Erin Duffy, Mom of 2*

One Thing

"Take time to do one thing for yourself each day. It doesn't matter how small or grand, but it matters that you do that one thing for you."

—*Christine J Boozer, Mom of 3*

34

Awareness

"Awareness is a Super Power! I work exclusively with Mothers. From their Maternity session forward, I discuss the importance of tapping into their awareness and instincts as a Mother. The first key to using your awareness is to trust and accept that this tool is there to help guide you. Like a compass that lives on the inside. Those nudges, whispers, and pulls are the awareness within. They're telling you to pay attention, listen up, and trust your instincts. The more you are accepting and embracing of them, the more it strengthens and your awareness can be the most valuable tool as a Mom."

—Deanna Ryan, Mom of 3

Understand Expectations

"Try not to set unrealistic expectations. Learn what is age-appropriate behavior. For example...Don't expect a toddler to sit still for hours. Toddlers, especially boys need exercise. Think about taking parenting classes, spend time with other moms, and learn what is age-appropriate."

—Dale L'Ecuyer, Mom of 5

"Without appreciating your opportunity of motherhood, you'll miss out on experiencing extraordinary emotions and growth individually and alongside your children."

—Susan Vernicek, Mom of twins

Chapter Two

Embrace Appreciation

Be Grateful and Celebrate

Each of us must develop an earnest appreciation for all that comprises our inner and outer lives—in motherhood and beyond. This encompasses gratitude for who we are, how we mature every day, and what we have reaped, despite obstacles that we encounter as women, in general, but certainly as mothers. Once we become thankful (internalize it and greet its cousin, compassion) we can genuinely celebrate our incomparable selves. In discovering our distinctive values, we are invested with an almost intuitive respect for them. And perhaps it's precisely then that we begin to fathom the endless possibilities. This kind of gratitude becomes part of the fuel that drives us as we navigate the oft-choppy waters of the motherhood domain.

Appreciate and Invigorate

In order to cultivate appreciation (again, a process) we must be mindful. The conscious mother must continually be aware (and, remember, self-accepting) of the layers of her personal, professional, and of course, the role of mother. We can reflect upon our feelings and observations. We can focus on external forces (including other individuals such as family, friends, competitors, colleagues, and yes, mothers) that impact us and upon which our actions have effect. Essentially, we can be grateful for both causes and effects, not to mention every seemingly small event we enjoy as we tread into and through the motherhood world. Establishing our value as women and Mothers, a pure appreciation naturally follows. And then it's time to rejoice!

Appreciation does not necessarily arise automatically or easily, particularly when what lies ahead can be overwhelming, scary, stressful—daunting even. It just might take some gentle nurturing. As counterintuitive as it can appear initially, obstacles and adversity can morph into gratitude if we slightly shift our vantage points. And since "challenge or putting out fires" may be the Mother's middle name, appreciation becomes yet a more prized aspiration.

Perhaps the shared wisdom and perspectives of the other mothers will instill or underscore a sense of gratitude within and without the daily running of our lives. Let them stroke our sense of appreciation. Let them light up our celebrations.

The Awareness Motherhood Demanded + The Appreciation it Delivered to Me

As I sit here typing away, I'm playing the nursery playlist that I had on replay almost 24/7 for the twins. It brings tears to my eyes listening and reminiscing on the good times, the struggles, and challenges of motherhood back then. Listening to the harmony of the beats brings me back to when I'd hold two newborns in my arms rocking them back and forth. And now I laugh because there's a whole new set of struggles and obstacles that I manage day-to-day. I'm sure you can relate, right?

What I do know now, only five years into motherhood, is that we must accept and embrace the entire journey because we may not appreciate all of the moments—in the moment, but we will always appreciate as we reflect back.

The goal for myself and my intention for all of you, my mother friends, is to wake up now, appreciate now, appreciate yesterday, and commit to appreciating tomorrow because feeling pure joy and abundance is attached at the hip to appreciation.

I appreciate the random tantrums my June and Cade throw my way. I appreciate the sound of the refrigerator door opening every five minutes because they want a snack. Soon they'll be off exploring and living their lives and I'll miss that little sound. These are the little things that we can take for granted. Since I started to journal, that's when I started to become more appreciative and aware of all the little gems motherhood gives us. It's a time to dig deep, reflect and create those lasting memories. One of the best pieces of advice I could offer another mother is to write, journal, and create those memories along the way. It not only deepens the memory, but you'll have something to go back to later.

It's your turn now. Appreciation is everything. What have you learned to appreciate about yourself and motherhood, physically and mentally?

Every Stage

"If I could go back 20 years and give myself advice, this is what I would say. As a mom, at every stage, we will have good days and bad days. We will have chaotic days and blissful days. We will have days that we lock ourselves in the bathroom just to get a minute alone, or to cry our eyes out. We will have days when we cry tears of joy for our child. It is easy to wish it all away, to focus on other things that tug at our attention, but don't. Appreciate every minute of it, because while it feels like you will be in this place forever, they grow up in the blink of an eye."

—*Donna Leyens, Mom of 2*

Believe

"Hey mom, believe me; your baby is grateful for everything you are doing. Keep showing up and don't give up."

—*Zaneta Chylewska, Mom of 1*

The Front Lines

"Being a mother is hard, and it can be thanklessly lonely at times. Remind yourself, when you're covered in spit up, haven't showered in 48 hours, are being manipulated by your little cutie pie, or screamed at by your teen, that you are doing the work that lays the foundation for the future. You're on the front lines. You are brave. Take a moment to appreciate and remind yourself of your intelligence, spirit, sense of humor, whatever aspects of yourself are being muffled by exhaustion. Remind yourself that you're still whole, and appreciate the important work you're doing every second of the day. Appreciate the strength that it takes. You are truly powerful, even when you are feeling the opposite."

—Dori Eldridge Bell, Mom of 1

Believe

"Don't quit on self-love, life, and all the experiences you deserve!"

—Susan Vernicek, Mom of Twins

Appreciate Each Stage

"Being a mom is one of the best jobs in the world. Sometimes we lose perspective. When your kids are little, you can't wait for them to be able to do more for themselves. When they are teenagers, you wish they would let you do more for them. Please stop and take the time to appreciate where they are at each stage of their growth and development. You've created these amazing beings. Live in the joy of their lives as they are happening. Be present to and for them."

—*Elizabeth Girouard, Mom of 3*

Respect + Appreciate

"Make sure they are fed healthy foods, limit sugar, drink water, get adequate sleep and EXERCISE. Those factors impact their behavior in a big way. Teach them to respect their body's needs at an early age."

—*Dale L'Ecuyer, Mom of 5*

You're the Student

"Don't pay as much attention to the advice of experts as you do to your own intuition. Before any of you came to the planet, you each chose the other—child and mother—to learn lessons and grow together. There is a good chance your child is more your teacher, than student.

The pressure you feel to mold, shape or fix your child is mostly an illusion. Don't worry about what you "should" do to be a good mom. Do what feels right to you. Yes it will get messy and it will feel scary sometimes. Listening to experts and following their rules can give us a temporary sense of "getting it right" but at the end of the day the truth about what will work for you, and your child, in your family resides in you and only you. Trust that. I say this having rigidly followed the advice of experts for 12 years. It was only when I freed myself of that completely that I found peace and ease and abundant love inside motherhood."

—*Patty Lennon, Mom of 2*

Many Hats

"I have learned to appreciate the many hats that I wear as a mother. It has taken me a bit to become appreciative. In stressful times, we often forget the "beginning" and its happiness. I once had a person say to me, "Remember, you prayed for this." It really convicted me. I took that comment and applied it to all areas of my life—the husband, the job, and the children. Let's face it, all three of the above can drive us crazy from time-to-time, LOL.

I've learned (and continue to learn) to pick my battles. My grandmother used to say that *"when they are small, they are small problems. And when they are big, they are big problems."* I'm still not sure how I feel about that, but if anything, it puts more of an emphasis on "molding" my kids with character, empathy, humility, and a hard work ethic right now. From what I'm told, these years fly by and tomorrow I will wish that my boys were still drawing on things, clogging toilets, and shooting the dogs with nerf guns. As of lately, I have felt the need to appreciate the "present." Some people don't get it, but I will often make everything stop so that we can have family time. My husband is an executive chef and works many long hours. It's important to pull the brakes and "just be" sometimes—not with anyone else's family, just ours. I appreciate that I can recognize what is needed for my family, and I am no longer bothered by those who just think we are being antisocial. Simply prioritizing our family above others—is not in a mean way, but because it's what we need to be effective and thrive together."

—Jaime Goulet, Mom of 2

Hold Your Baby

"Hold your baby often. Rest when your baby sleeps. One thing I know from experience, you'll be a more patient mom if you're well-rested as much as possible."

—Dale L'Ecuyer, Mom of 5

Slow Down

"With three kids, and in general, I feel that I'm rushing to rush ALL THE TIME! Always thinking of "to-dos" or "next-up" on the agenda. I've even found myself telling the kids all too often to "hurry up" or do things faster or quicker...but this was always stemmed from my lack of preparation. So, take the extra time to plan and let your kids be kids...because we all know time flies and some day soon, you will say wait, slow down!"

—Jennifer Schumacher, Mom of 3

Cherish

"It's all the "lasts" that I'm grateful to have. The last breast feeding, the last bath in the sink, the last diaper change, the last. You get the idea. I encourage to cherish them all!"

—Jami Josephson Chace, Mom of 1

Friendship

"Motherhood will keep you busy. Sometimes too busy where you don't remember to check in on your friends. Never lose appreciation for great friendship, and I encourage you to even go as far as setting a reminder in your phone to either text or call your friends monthly. Even if you're the one making most of the calls and check-ins, it's OK, there's always a leader between friendships. Be the leader so you don't lose touch."

—Susan Vernicek, Mom of Twins

Embrace Crazy

"Every day I'm thankful to have two amazing children that lighten my heart at the sound of their voices. I don't mind the mess, I don't mind the crazy, and I don't mind the emotion, because they make me be a better person—and a better mother."

—*Theresa Mary Hudzinski, Mom of 2*

Smell the Roses

"With my first son, every cry rattled me to the core with anxiety. When he grew out of the baby stage, I felt regret and heart break that I didn't stop to smell the roses. With my second son, I took the time to smile and relish each cry, each explosive diaper, whatever the case was because I knew I would miss it all. Taking control of what you appreciate makes life a little sweeter, because after all these emotions we feel, are simply just in our head. Our happiness is of course a choice, not always easy, but the hardest choices have the best rewards. The ability to change one's mind leads to the sweet reward of self growth, that of which we are all truly striving for in our lives."

—*Erin Duffy, Mom of 2*

Who They Are

"Appreciate your children for who they are, not for who you want them to be."

—Christine J Boozer, Mom of 3

Opportunity

"Within the chaos lies opportunity. You're thinking, "yea right" or "NO way!" When you find yourself spinning out of control or feeling like you're losing it; sit down and ground yourself. You can make a choice to get caught up in the spiraling effect and let the chaos tangle you all up or choose to appreciate the chaos and surrender to it. Right there, as you sit, whether it's in your car, your living room, bathroom, bedroom or desk at work, think of five things you're grateful for. There is opportunity in the chaos, there lies gratitude in every moment. IF we only make the choice to see it, embrace it and accept it and appreciate it."

—Deanna Ryan, Mom of 3

"Mama, promise me you'll always celebrate your daily wins!"

—Susan Vernicek, Mom of Twins

Chapter Three

How to Achieve

...mplish and Triumph

...ig other nifty gifts, these quotes will remind you ...at first, any advancement is an achievement. Every day that you choose to wake is an achievement. Every single day you raise your children you're succeeding. The truth is that victories manifest in many forms. For the Mother, getting dressed, loving their children the best they can, laughing with them, reading to them, cleaning them, feeding them, finding their matching sock, putting toothpaste on their toothbrush, putting that dollar bill under their pillows—are all incremental feats worthy of note and pride. Every such effort, no matter how outwardly teensy, is an action taken toward growth and fulfillment. Enthusiasm, commitment, and consistency make the most diminutive accomplishments go the distance toward greater wins.

We're aiming for abundance, rather than perfection. (Is perfection a realistic attainment in any regard?) It behooves us to seek to excite and satisfy ourselves. Concern about how others gauge "good mothering" is a waste of precious time and already busy brain cells.

Succeeding in motherhood is not equal, it's subjective. As you will soon read, mothers attest that the love ranks the highest when it comes to feeling proud and raising children. Ultimately, reaching a harmonious balance between all of the roles of motherhood and being, ya know, human, is the winning tick. And that's all up to your ability to be conscious, aware and accepting your success in the now.

Failure schmailure. Remember that failure is merely a perception: almost always a subjective construct generated by attitude and belief. Even a scenario we immediately presume to be a letdown or down-right flop can potentially be re-purposed as a lesson learned and turned toward further development, or repackaged (like a gift). It is a detour that reroutes us toward even greater reward. Each experience becomes intrinsic to the adventure of the determined mother, who must steadfastly forge her own path through a series of focused efforts. By adapting and evolving, we thereby create our abundance and our harmonious balance.

Full circle, here we come. As evidenced by many of the quotes in *Get All A's in the Game of Life*, once we assent and celebrate, the horizon widens for a deeper experience of satisfaction. Considering all we have to contend with in and out of motherhood, us moms stack our achievements from the instant we awaken to tackle each day. When we proceed to marry our "haves" and "must dos" with passion and resourcefulness, well, abundance is ours for the tak-ing. And, Moms, that means prosperity, not matter how we slice it!

℩ I Started Achieving as a Mother

s the first night out of the hospital and at my ..om's house because she was closer to the hospital. I could only bring one of my babies home, June. Cade had to stay a few days in the NICU to gain some more weight.

We tried everything, rocking, feeding, and we even tried building June a cozy crib in a dresser drawer. Nothing would stop her crying and I was exhausted. I remember laying in bed with my mom as she tried and kept calm for all 3 of us. My husband was staying at the hospital and I was so glad I had my mom because all I could think of was how I couldn't have done that on my own. I thought I was failing already on day one.

When it was time to go home, which was an hour away from the hospital and family, I was scared. I had another "first" night to get through as a mother of two—twins none-the-less. That night was hell, I'm not going to lie. Hours of screaming and I was stressed for so many reasons because my husband had to work the next day and I was worried he'd wake up. Um, well, no, soon discovered he is a very sound sleeper and didn't budge. I cursed him out for sure, I divorced him in my head while I was trying to nurse two babies at the same time. I crack up thinking about how crazy that night was and how delirious my mind was.

That was the night I started to achieve as a mother. I started to believe I was capable because I was doing it, I was taking care of two babies all night long and I didn't run out the front door. That memory gives me power and evidence of how capable I am of being a great mother.

Now, I can honestly share that I almost NEVER struggle with comparison syndrome when it comes to being a great Mother. I know many mothers struggle with comparing and it strips us of our current joy and appreciation. I would say it's because of all the personal development work that I do and know that I am showing up the best I know how to every day while at the same time, pushing myself to grow and do better for not just myself, but for my children and family.

I own and embrace my mom skills and effort and that's what's important. YOU and only YOU need to be proud and know that you're the best mother for your children. Right?

I know you'll do whatever it takes to bring joy and give your children the best opportunities and experiences. Therefore, you won't lose my friend. So remember, take on each day knowing you are already succeeding in motherhood. You're already achieving by the time you say yes to the new day, right?

ᵖ taking those daily efforts and remember the
ᵐportant aspect of being a Mother, is loving
ₑlf and your family. Love always wins.

Your turn! What are your most rewarding achievements in motherhood? Journal what makes YOU most proud, and what goals and dreams that you still have and would like to reach for yourself and for your children.

End of Night Win

"I tell my daughter every night before bed that she is smart, strong, kind, funny, and beautiful. I always say beautiful last in hopes that I instill in her that there are so many other qualities that are equally, if not more important. #burnyourbra"

—*Victoria Ronemus, Mom of 1*

When Exhausted

"It can be really hard to see achievement when you're physically and emotionally exhausted, so some days the achievement bar will be skimming the ground (everyone is still alive) and other days the bar will be up over your head (who knocked this Motherhood thing out of the park today? I did!) Both are perfectly acceptable."

—*Dori Eldridge Bell, Mom of 1*

Proof

"Your smiling baby is proof that you are doing everything fine."

—*Zaneta Chylewska, Mom of 1*

You've Got This

"Each day is a blessing. When it seems like you can't do anything right, have compassion for yourself. You are exactly where you are meant to be. Think of ONE thing you did right and remember, you've got this!!"

—*Elizabeth Girouard, Mom of 3*

Communicate

"Don't assume others, especially your partner, knows what you need. Learn to communicate quickly and direct with the exact help and support you need."

—*Susan Vernicek, Mom of Twins*

Trust

"I think the most important thing I've learned as a Mother is to trust your instincts. Really, they are usually right!"

—*Jami Josephson Chace, Mom of 1*

Embrace the 24/7

"Motherhood is a 24/7 job, the hardest job on the planet, but the most rewarding. It will take many years to really see the fruits of your labor. Know that all the work you put into your children in the early years will set the stage for the rest of your lives."

—*Dale L'Ecuyer, Mom of 5*

Productive & Effective

"I had my daughter during one of the most stressful times in my life. I needed to be 120 percent present in my job in a foreign country. If I did not have my children, I'm not sure I could have made it through. At the time, my daughter taught me— or rather forced me to step back and let go. I could only do so much and within my control. And I discovered that being present in the moment actually makes you more productive and effective."

—*Theresa Mary Hudzinski, Mom of 2*

Do What Feels Right

"Don't pay as much attention to the advice of experts as you do to your own intuition. Before any of you came to the planet you each chose the other—child and Mother—to learn lessons and grow together. There is a good chance your child is more your teacher, than student. The pressure you feel to mold, shape or fix your child is mostly an illusion. Don't worry about what you "should" do to be a good mom. Do what feels right to you.

Yes it will get messy and it will feel scary sometimes. Listening to experts and following their rules can give us a temporary sense of "getting it right" but at the end of the day the truth about what will work for you, and your child, in your family resides in you and only you. Trust that. I say this having rigidly followed the advice of experts for 12 years. It was only when I freed myself of that completely that I found peace and ease and abundant love inside Motherhood."

—*Patty Lennon, Mom of 2*

Mothering With Intentionality

"I am often my worst critic; therefore, this area is an ongoing process. I take "Mothering" very seriously. I was told I would not have children based off poor decisions/choices made from the ages of 17-23 years old. I count it a miracle from God that I have two healthy (and wild) boys. It was my mission since the beginning to raise my children well. My children would know structure, be encouraged, have a Mother and father that loved and showed this to each other, understand that they are fearfully and wonderfully made, and would always live in a safe environment. My greatest achievement thus far is that I am Mothering with "intentionality." I've always taken on the responsibility to make changes in my family lineage. My parents did the best they could in the circumstances presented; however, come hell or high water—I would not allow those circumstances to repeat.

I know there will be trials and problems that arise; however, I (personally) take comfort in scripture and a personal relationship with Jesus. Prayers ground me, refocus my thoughts, and give me motivation and encouragement to keep pushing though the difficult times. *I need all the help I can get!"*

—*Jaime Goulet, Mom of 2*

Own Your Dreams

"Dreams + Effort = Goals Accomplished. Yes, you're a Mother, but your dreams and desires still matter. So go create your dream list and create those 5-10 actions steps and start taking them one-by-one, day-by-day. All you need are a few steps to get you started and the momentum will follow. With the constant forward action, no matter how tiny you may think, you will reach your goals eventually."

—*Susan Vernicek, Mom of Twins*

Achieving With Bread Crumbs

"Sometimes dinner can lead to our biggest achievements and failures in our day-to-day with kids. Creating a new recipe from what you have left in your pantry sounds silly to relate achievement to. However, when you're budgeting for your family, trying not to be wasteful, and keeping everyone happy, it's actually a tough job. Sometimes looking outside the box, making a plan, and then executing it with happy faces and full bellies can make any mom feel like they climbed Mt. Everest. Out of bread crumbs? No worries, create a new recipe the kids will love like cheese and crackers coated chicken. Use up what you have in the pantry, save money, sanity, and give yourself some damn credit!"

—*Erin Duffy, Mom of 2*

You're the Super Hero

"Self-love is a big thing for me. I have become a much better mom since I started taking care of myself and loving myself. It brings a sense of calmness and peace to my life. When the chaos comes and your world is crashing down around you, it's OK to take some time to yourself. By taking this time to decompress, to center yourself, and focus, you are showing your children how to cope and face adversity, how to rise up after you have been knocked down, how to face your fears and become stronger. You are showing your children that it's OK, not to be OK. Take that moment to yourself, but don't stay down long. Rise up and kick ass, because there are better days ahead and you're going to be ready, grateful, and graceful! You are worthy, you are loved, and you are raising strong children to have healthy coping mechanisms. There have been times I have locked myself in the bathroom for 1 minute (those kids notice when mom is gone, sometimes you don't have much time), breathe and center yourself. That minute will help you refocus on where you need to be. Slow down, cuddle your children, take care of yourself. You can't keep on giving pieces of yourself if you don't take the time to fill your cup up. No one else can fill that cup, so make sure you have your own back. By taking care of yourself, you are taking care of your children, they will see a happier mom, who is strong, and faces the world no matter what the circumstances are. You are their super hero! Own that shit!"

—Maria Frascella, Mom of 2

Choices

"Make sure to separate the action from the child meaning the child isn't BAD, the action may not have been the best choice. Teach them to be in control of themselves, not by scolding, but by giving them choices and LOGICAL consequences."

—Dale L'Ecuyer, Mom of 5

You'll Feel Proud

"It'll all work out and you'll feel proud. Start embracing that feeling sooner than later."

—Doris Vernicek Mom of 3

You Can

"You can handle so much more than you think you can."

—Christine J Boozer, Mom of 3

It's Okay to Nap

"It's OK to take a nap. Just because you nap, doesn't mean you're not a great Mother. The nap is actually helping you be a great Mother. I used to feel so guilty taking a 20-minute nap while the twins watched a Disney show. It's just what I call, thought drama. Creating thoughts that don't serve me at all and create internal struggle. So take that nap and be a refreshed Mother, my friend."

—Susan Vernicek, Mom of Twins

Tool Box

"I think of Motherhood as being the builder of a tool box for each of my children. Each child is unique and requires their own specific toolbox. Having three boys, they each bring three very different personalities to the family dynamic. For example, our oldest Jack is the kindest soul, patient, understanding, puts a lot of pressure upon himself to try to be perfect, achieves great grades, and is an awesome athlete too. So in his tool box, I have included journals with prompts written by me to help him get out of over thinking and just writing his thoughts/feelings. I have given him tools to help master his anxious/nervous energy. He has become a master of listening to calming music, or watching waterfalls to ground himself. He knows how to deep breathe to calm himself. He is an avid reader, so I have included books next to his bed to help teach him about becoming a young man with lots of lessons about acceptance, being resilient, and determined.

I monitor what he is reading and looking at and I make sure (as much as possible) that he is following positive, inspirational, motivational and faith-filled content. His toolbox is always there when he needs it to open and use when he needs guidance or direction."

—Deanna Ryan, Mom of 3

Build Self-Esteem

"The most important thing you can do for your child is to build their self-esteem. What that means is to allow them to be who they are—especially with 6 kids."

—*Mama Bear, Mom of 6*

Small Wins

"Celebrate the small wins every single day and you will always feel a sense of accomplishment."

—*Donna Leyens, Mom of 2*

Comparing

"When you stop comparing your life and parenting style, you'll starting winning every day as a Mother. Don't waste your precious energy on those kind of thoughts. You are amazing as a human and a Mother."

—*Susan Vernicek, Mom of Twins*

Bonus

Mom Articles

Over the years, I've written a few pieces about motherhood. This is section has a few of those articles I've written for my digital magazine about motherhood.

So, I thought it would be great to include them in here for you as well. I hope you enjoy them and I hope they bring you some laughter, comfort, and inspiration.

Please know that if you are ever interested in sharing your stories, experiences, or advice, I'd love to have you share with our readers on my digital magazine, IdentityMagazine.net.

To keep things really direct, all you have to do is email Editor@identitymagazine.net and reference this book and we can take the next step.

The Night Before Kindergarten

It was the night before Kindergarten and we're all so very excited. Especially mama because her free time is about to ignite!

June and Cade ask Alexa to wake them up in the AM. Me, oh mama me, smirks and thinks about that afternoon nap—because I can.

We've conquered the school prep with such joy. Double the haircuts, double the clothes, double the shoes and I'm thinking oh boy.

We picked out our deli cuts, cheese cubes, and fruits. We stocked up on snacks, gummy bears, but couldn't find any Barbaloots.

We definitely had a dance party, we're all super excited. I'm so sorry that you all weren't invited.

It was shake your booty, twist, and shout, and I won't forget Cade's belly break dance until his pants dropped out.

They brushed their teeth, rinsed with mouthwash— and I just thought, oh my gosh.

They are 5.

They dress themselves.

They wipe themselves.

They brush their teeth and rinse and repeat.

All by themselves.

It's the night before kindergarten and I'm beside my-self. We've entered the next chapter but, ugh there's still Elf on the Shelf.

To all a good night, I'm about to ignite, this mama here is starting tonight!

Thanks for reading my random poem/rhyme— it just came to me, probably because of the wine.

xoxo

I wanted to include this poem because it was a moment of play and creativity that literally came to me after I tucked the twins into bed for the night before their first day. Remember to let go, play, dance and celebrate with your children.

Susan Vernicek, Mom of Twins

What Motherhood is all About

I've got a little birth story for ya and some inspiration for ya.

It was the morning of and I was pretty calm. So calm that I took my "38-weeks, today is the day!" selfie photo and Rob and I went on our way. We had a long hour drive to get to our hospital where I'd be induced around 9:00 AM.

Both of us still pretty darn calm as we got settled into the room. We whipped out our laptop and starting finishing our Dexter Netflix binge.

Honestly, I still pray my twins are not serial killers from Rob and I watching, not 2, 3 or 4 hours of Dexter, but EIGHT (8) hours of that show. LOL, we laugh to this day about that.

I had maybe an hour of extraordinary pain because I said no to the epidural and then when I wanted it, I had to wait for the doc to return, which was an hour + later. So I dropped a few F-bombs and tried not to think about killing Rob while I was being tortured—oh, good times.

It was about 8:45 PM when I was taken to an operating room, for a vaginal delivery. And because I was having twins, it had to be in an operating room just in case.

I was surrounded by doctors and Rob had to stand by my head, which was better for him because he almost passes out every time he sees blood or needles. *So weak, I say with humor internally. HA!*

Next thing I know I had one baby, Baby A, which was June. I swear, I didn't feel a thing and didn't even know I was pushing, LOL. Then 14 minutes later, Baby Cade came screaming his way out and now the two of them are complete opposites. June is the loud one and Cade is calm and cool.

Here's the thing, when it comes to Motherhood, I hang onto the confidence I had while carrying the twins for 9 months and delivering them that day. I took care of myself the best I could and took action in preparing myself the best I could without getting wrapped up in too much of "what to expect."

Frankly, I expected it was going to be hard as sh*t to carry twins for 9 months, deliver, and be a Mother. And, I expected motherhood was going to take soooo much effort, strength, emotions, fear, love— every ounce of emotion and being out of me. I was confident in that, accepted it, and am still embracing the "hard as sh*t effort."

In my belief or opinion, Motherhood is all about our own confidence.

Sure, we are human and confidence is a muscle to

be worked. But boy, it feels so good when you grab a hold of your very own and conquer your world with it.

Are ya with me?

What gives us confidence?

Belief, action, and knowledge give us confidence in motherhood, relationships, career, and everything we will experience.

Since being a mother, one of the biggest things I've had to work on is confidence. It seems that every situation, circumstance, struggle, or fear that I experience—it always leads back to a lack of confidence.

When I feel that lack of confidence, I think about my belief at that moment I reflect on what kind of actions I can take and what knowledge can I learn to gain the confidence I need.

It all comes down to YOU and YOUR MIND.

Motherhood can be scary, but if you believe that you'll take all the action necessary to achieve and do your best, then you should have confidence. Right?

Do you trust and believe that you'll do what it takes?

I have no fear in the way I parent because I know I'm doing the best I can with what I know every single day. I push to learn more so I have the knowledge and take more action so I build belief and strengthen my confidence every single day as the curve balls come my way.

I've been saying this for years. Confidence is not a destination, motherhood is not a destination, love is not a destination, belief is not a destination—It's all a journey and muscles to be worked.

And nobody should feel alone on this journey—we should all have support without judgment from others.

Mom Turns Down Book of the Month

I was a Kindergarten Mom for less than two months and I had already been challenged with obstacles from packing the right lunches, to dropping my kids off at the right door, to making choices not to participate in certain activities we don't agree with.

I'll be honest in sharing that I'm not excited about all the future additional decisions that come with having kids in school. However, I know I must accept, own and embrace the experiences as best as I can so that I continue to grow along with our children.

Our elementary school offered a great program for the students. It's something called, one book, one school where the entire school (in our case K-5) read the same book. Well, the book they chose was Maltida. I'm very familiar and love the story, but I was shocked that this was picked for the parents to read to kindergartners.

The Stink Eye

My husband and I gave it a try, of course. But within the first few pages, my husband and I kept catching ourselves giving each other the "what the heck stink eyes." It didn't feel right, it didn't feel appropriate.

Many of the words we were reading, our 5-year-old twins were hearing for the first time. Idiot, dumb, stupid and much more—I didn't want those teachable moments to be forced like that, let alone out of our mouths first.

It just felt off for both of us and we decided to inform the teacher that we were going to pick another book to read. We were both nervous, and of course, feared judgment because it's only human to second guess parenting. And...we didn't want their teacher to think we were going to be the pain in the ass parents, LOL.

Proud

Now, it feels soo good that we made that decision and we actually picked an amazing book to read. I gotta say how proud I feel to be able to follow my intuition and go for it. To actually implement the desires I've been envisioning to implement as a parent for years. There have been so many things I said, I was going to do and never did, so I'm finally doing something, HA! Like yearly Santa photos, um nope, didn't even get one.

My Childhood

Growing up I remember attending church, going to Sunday School and using that Aunt Jamima looking glue. Until one day, we stopped. From my memory, it was after my grandmother passed that we stopped going (my Father's Mom). From then, religion wasn't part of our childhood, nor my adulthood.

Rock Bottom

Until I hit rock bottom— a few times. Over a decade ago I started taking the steps to heal and have now found happiness, inner peace, love, and success. I even have a new connection to the Universe, God and/or that Higher Power that some of us refer to.

Changing Patterns

I've decided to change the patterns for my children, and my husband is on board too. I recently read *The Universe Has Your Back by Gabrielle Bernstein* and it shifted my love, belief and trust paradigm— big time.

Sometimes I chant "The Universe Has My Back" throughout the day as I manage to run a business, nurture my children, take care of the house and keep a healthy relationship with my husband. Sometimes, you need all the support you can get, right?

So that's the book we decided to read to our twins and they're loving it so far. We have conversations about love, God, The Universe, and mantras to help calm ourselves down when we're feeling frustrated.

They get to learn about fear, faith, love, angels and speaking the truth, and I'm loving their expressions as I read it to them. In time, they'll read Maltida, but for now, I want to read, teach and nurture them a book that as a family, we will grow and strengthen our minds together.

This minor choice seemed so big to my husband and I that it gave me a "badass mom" kinda feeling. And I'll take those moments of success and badass as often as I can. Wouldn't you?

I've made a little list of a few random thoughts and wins, according to me of course.

I (my husband and I), made a parenting choice together and feel even more connected because of these new experiences we are having as a team. It seems so silly, but these moments are creating more magic between us.

I feel like the leader I want to be by teaching my kids important mental health, self-love, trust, and belief as early as possible.

There will always be judgers and haters. I know this and I know that it has nothing to do with me.

I will also respect the teachers and school, while at the same time voice my concerns and do the best I can with what I know and how I see the situation. I'm going to stand proud and strong in teaching my kids love, kindness, trust, and all about the Universe and God so that they feel comfortable and knowledgeable.

Us Moms, all of us do the best we know how to at any given moment and experience. I must remember progress will always be tied to parenting, not perfection.

I'd love to hear how you're owning and embracing motherhood, and if you have any tips for a newbie kindergarten Mom, feel free to share.

Actions and Exercises You Can Take for Children's Mental Health Awareness

Part of the work I love is supporting mental health and if we can start supporting our children's mental health at a young age, even better. Here are some ideas that have helped me over the years.

Appreciation/Gratitude

Having an appreciation for the little and the big things in life—is proven to broaden our mental health. There are many studies and there's scientific evidence that when you practice gratitude DAILY, more happiness and abundance shows up within your life.

Real happiness, creates a stronger and more positive mental state. If we can practice this with our children, as early as we start reading to them, I believe it will set them up for mental strength and positive awareness—just like your children may say their prayers at night, follow up with all that they are grateful for from their day.

Even if it's the light in their room, get them in a routine to practice and teach them that everything in life is truly a gift. Children are our future and we are responsible to teach and guide them. Wouldn't you agree?

Compassion

Show yourself, and not just your children, all children daily compassion, love, caring, authenticity, laughter and more! Let yourself and provide them the experience that every emotion (good and bad) have to offer.

I encourage you to teach yourself and them ways to heal, think, and problem solve. We can't ignore ourselves, and of course, our children.

Let's engage and speak positive and supportive to ourselves and our children and others. It doesn't matter how old or young others are, we must lead by example with kindness and respect and our children will follow.

Support

Find a circle of support who believe in a positive lifestyle for their families as well. Nothing in life is easy, so be sure to have a support team in place for when you need help in any way. There is no shame, trust me.

Get All A's

Remember that we set examples; they watch everybody's moves. Practice kindness and think about Identity's mission and message of getting all A's in your game of life. Take every Moment and think about acceptance, appreciation, and achieving.

Each Moment is a teachable Moment. How will you make a difference for your mental health and our children's mental health? Mental Health plays a vital role within our identities. Our mental wellbeing is probably the most difficult muscle to exercise. One thing I do know is that it's never, never too late to practice, teach, and learn.

I'm Not a Bad Mom, I'm a Badass Mom

When was the last time you reflected on what an awesome job you're doing being a Mom? I bet you spend more time feeling guilty and believing you're a bad Mom relatively often, right?

I found several statistics on how we Moms allow guilt to creep into our lives. *Working Mother Research Institute* surveyed over 3,700 women and issued a report called, *"What Moms Choose."**

51 percent of working mothers feel guilty about not spending enough time with their children:*

We need to get over this already and begin focusing on the time that we do get to spend with our children. Create the goal to make the time you do have the best time and the most fun—in other words, be present. I feel that I'm always hearing, "I want and I need more time" and it's not only with children. This can center on many other tasks or circumstances in life.

Try to make a priority list every day of what you want most to accomplish. Do your best throughout the day and later, don't beat yourself up over it.

Seriously, almost all of us work and NONE of us can compare our family situations with the next person's. You may have more spare time in the summer if you are a teacher, or maybe you're a coach and not available during a particular season, but have more time during the other months. Or maybe your work is 4 days on and 4 days off.

Every day I aim for these:

Make sure my kids laugh hysterically, even if it's just by tickling them.

Be sure to feed myself and my family something super healthy.

Be sure to drink water and ensure that my kids do too.

Indulge myself in something I enjoy.

Kiss my husband and children so much that I'm like the annoying Mom from The Goldbergs.

Make sure I say "I love you" multiple times a day.

It's that simple. Those are the most important elements in life, right? Not money, not bills, not material things-but rather laughter, love, affection, respect and trying one's best.

55 percent of working mothers feel guilt about the untidiness of their house*

Okay, I can totally relate to this because I do have a slight case of OCD. However, I've really come a long way over that during the past two years raising twins. What I do know is: I strive to clean 1 room a day and I don't berate myself if I don't necessarily accomplish that. For the most part, thinking this way and implementing this 1 room a day approach has had a tremendous impact on my family and stress levels because I'm not obsessed and trying to clean the entire house every day.

49 percent of working mothers and 47 percent of stay-at-home-mothers agreed with the statement, "I am my worst critic"*

STOP! Switch the mindset to "I am a badass Mom and my family is lucky to have me." Stop acknowledging that "I am my worst critic." There is no need to judge ourselves because there are plenty of other people doing that for us.

So, we need to step into our confidence, own our badass Mom roles and continue to do our best and leave the judging to the rest (without letting that effect us either, since this is also in our control).

I've gathered some quotes/statements from other badass Moms and I hope they inspire you to recognize how badass you are!

"I'm a badass Mom because I will do anything in my power to keep my children safe and happy. And if I have to hurt someone doing that, so be it."
—Evelyn Rosas

"I'm a badass Mom because I'm teaching my kids that failure only happens when you're too afraid to try. And that their dreams deserve a chance and that the only opinion that matters is their own opinion of themselves. I'm teaching them that every step towards faith and away from fear is a step in the right direction. I'm teaching them that the only way to truly love others is to love yourself first. I'm teaching them how being in love with yourself and content with who you are is the most freeing feeling in the world. I'm creating an army of people who won't wait for permission to be amazing—who will love openly and readily and never fear what's next because they know they are enough and the Universe and their Mom will always have their back. That's why I'm a badass Mom." —Bridget Irvy

"I'm a badass Mom because I've taught my kids how to be independent, especially when it comes to their own incomes. My son ran his own chewing gum business for years and my daughter has her own YouTube channel. I love that! They enjoy helping me create content for my courses, they listen when I practice my talks and my daughter is even the voice of my podcast introduction. I'm so grateful that my son sees me speak from the stage about

women and money, and our right to create our own destinies. I'm raising my kids who believe the sky's the limit and who know that women are an important part of the business world."
—Sarah Walton

"I'm a badass Mom because I taught my kids to be fearless by re-inventing myself and starting a whole new career! I'm a badass Mom because I chose what was best for them. I raised them to be strong and independent—even when that independence might (and did) lead them far away."
—Stephanie Dalfonzo

"I'm a badass Mom because I took a leap to start my own business. I'm not always home for dinner or bedtime. I plan events so I'm helping people celebrate. But my kids are clean, fed, loved, and we celebrate each success we have in a special way! I am showing "my body" a woman can be her own boss and have a happy family! Let's not forget the glass of wine accompanying me on my journey—LOL."
—Anita Belle

"When my first son was born, I tried to do everything 'right' and I was miserable. I loved my son more than anything, but I missed 'me.' I missed dressing up and wearing heels and going out with girlfriends. When my second son was born, I made the decision that I couldn't lose myself in motherhood.

I need to work, feel productive, and enjoy a social life outside of my home, in order to fully enjoy being a Mom. It's not easy or without the guilt, but everyone is happier for it."
—Vanessa Coppes

"Badass Moms love unconditionally with all their heart. Through happiness, fears, anger and tears; they do whatever is best for their children no matter what anyone else thinks. I'm a badass Mom because of this and I know you are too."
—Jodi Ciampa

"I am a badass Mom because I am showing my three sons how to live your life with passion and purpose. Sure, the house gets messy and dinner is not always homemade, but they have a Mom who is LIT UP doing what she loves. That to me is the most inspirational lesson." —Mallika Malhotra

End the guilt. You're not a bad Mom. You're a badass Mom, along with all Moms!

Here are a few reasons why I'm a badass Mom and I'm just blurting stuff out and being as authentic as I can—I'm owning me…

Party: I'm always up for a party. As long as I have a babysitter, I'm all in. I have NO shame or guilt when leaving my kids to go have fun with friends for a night. Being able to get out and dance, drink, and laugh, revitalizes my soul.

Dance party with my kids: I party with my kids on a weekly basis by dancing to videos and throughout the house while jumping on the couches and beds. I know how to balance my children's diet while **spoiling them** with sweets. Sometimes they get pancakes for dinner and sometimes they get cookies for breakfast.

I **still wear lingerie** and still have fun with my husband. It's not all about the kids ALL the time.

I **give 100%** every day and my goals for each day are to laugh, eat balanced, indulge, give lots of hugs and kisses to my twins and my husband.

I **practice being present** and mindful—consciously living and parenting the best I can.

I **run my own business** while being a wife, raising twins, and taking care of our home.

I **have a great sense of humor**—a sometimes inappropriate kind of humor to many, except my best friend and my brother-in-law.

I'm not afraid, nor feel guilty, when I have to travel for my career or have plans that don't involve my husband or kids. It's important for us to have our own space, as well as our quality time together.

I love **vodka + bloody marys.**

I love sex and **never make excuses** not to have it because of the kids. I'm a better, more relaxed Mom for it. (Sorry Mom) heeehee

I **love to love** and show that **love.**

I **lead by example** and teach my kids healthy eating, fitness, playing, humor, manners, respect and to love.

I'm not a bad Mom, I'm a badass Mom, just like you are. My question for you, how are you owning your Mom style?

2011 What Moms Choose Report: http://www.wmmsurveys. com/whatMomschoose.html (over 3700 participants)

Use the space below and keep this as a reminder. So when you pick this book up from time-to-time, you can remember why you're the best Mom for your children and feel proud of who you are.

Resources

For Moms

My Community + Books

Identitymagazine.net: A wellness community empowering women to transform through self-acceptance, appreciation and personal achievement—*Get All A's in the Game of Life*

Susanvernicek.com: Mindset Igniter + Coach, I teach women how to create a healthy internal dialogue so that they can reignite their energy and go from yelling "F... to F-Yeah!"

The Identity Magbook: Empowering you through stories from the first 3 years of Identity magazine while guiding you through the A-game and offering you an opportunity to journal. Susanvernicek.com/the-identity-magbook

Get All A's in the Game of Life: A series of books where women come together to share words of wisdom for the purpose of nurturing and motivating you ever forward. GetAllAs.com

Online Communities:

Jugglingthejenkins.com: Tiffany is a wife, mother, best-selling author, content creator and recovering addict. She's best known for her funny viral Facebook and YouTube videos, Tiffany is incredibly passionate about bringing awareness to mental illness.

Themombeat.com: The Mom Beat is a lifestyle, entertainment and humor site for moms discussing parenthood, pregnancy, family, pop culture, news, food, home decor, funny pictures and videos, and gems we find 'round the Web.

Sunshinemomma.com: A family lifestyle blog that covers topics relatable to the average family.

Believeinspiregrow.com: An organization and community where women are better together. B.I.G. supports women's entire lives.

Books that have helped, healed and inspired me:

"The How of Happiness" By Sonja Lyubomirsky
"Everything is Figureoutable" By Marie Forleo
"A Happy Pocket Full of Money" By Gikandi
"The Slight Edge" By Jeff Olsen
"Better than Before" By Gretchen Rubin
"The Four Agreements" By Don Miguel Ruiz
"The Gifts of Imperfection" By Brené Brown
"Girl, Wash Your Face" By Rachel Hollis
"The 5 Second Rule" By Mel Robbins
"Big Magic" By Elizabeth Gilbert
"The Universe Has My Back" By Gabriel Bernstein

These are my personal favorites and I'm not receiving compensation to feature them.

susan vernicek

Evolve With Empowerment + Results

identity magazine

xo Susan Vernicek

A Wellness Community Empowering Women to Transform Through
Self-Acceptance, Appreciation, and Personal Achievement—*Get All A's*™